SKY
FULL OF
STARS

HOW COMPARISON CAN KILL YOUR LIGHT

CHRÉTIEN
DUMOND

Sky Full of Stars: How Comparison Can Kill Your Light
Chrétien Dumond

Copyright © 2017 Chrétien Dumond

Famous Publishing
Austin, Texas

Library of Congress Control Number: 9781944187224

ISBN: 978-1-944187-22-4

Sky Full of Stars goes to the heart of addressing the real struggle of comparing ourselves to others. Chrétien's testimony on how to face your insecurities and embrace your true identity in Jesus is a must-read for anyone interested in being who God created him or her to be—and that includes all of us. Blessings above and beyond as you enjoy reading *Sky Full of Stars*!

Steve D. Holder
Lead Pastor of Bethel Church, Goldsboro, NC
President of The Fellowship Network, Dallas, TX

When I think of the author, Chrétien, I think of "one of a kind," which is really the truth he conveys in his inimitable way. Chrétien has translated his unique personality and personal journey into a story that is "one of a kind." He has a special gift to get us to believe in ourselves, tie that belief to our own uniqueness given by our Creator, and inspire us to believe that together we can do great things on our own journey through life.

Dr. David Robinson, PhD
Leadership Coach, Chicago, IL

READ THIS BOOK! Chrétien had me from the first page. Each of us aches to experience this life to the full. His humorous and honest writing will inspire and propel you to be all God created you to be. I LOVED reading *Sky Full Of Stars*!

Dr. Daryl Merrill Jr., PhD
Lead Pastor of Christian Life Church, Mt. Prospect, IL

SKY FULL OF STARS

I love Chrétien's transparency and vulnerability. Who hasn't struggled with comparisons? I've heard it said that comparing yourself to others is an insult to God, for He created you! Chrétien pointedly states that comparison can literally be deadly, and only distracts us from fulfilling the call of God on our lives. I love that Chrétien addresses this topic with insight and relevancy that this generation can understand. This topic affects everyone — and everyone should read this book.

Landon Schott
The Rev Ministries

WOW! With inspired vulnerability and transparency, Chrétien shares how comparison often leads to crippling struggles with insecurities. The truths found in this book will resonate in the hearts of men and women everywhere. Let's no longer be a generation that compares and competes! Let us celebrate and complete one another in our churches, homes, friendships, and even in our workplaces.

Beverly Weeks
Author, Speaker, and Director of the Wayne
Pregnancy Care Center of
Wayne County, NC

This book is must-read for the older generation. Chrétien lets us know that even in our later years, our dreams, aspirations, talents, and gifts can still be implemented as we continue to "Reach for the Stars." Add this book to your library!

Linda Moore
Senior Adult Ministry Director
Bethel Church, Goldsboro, NC

What an amazing book! It gives you a chance to become naked. Chrétien's transparency reminds me that all of us have questioned our existence and purpose more times than a few. Nevertheless, we have a purpose to fulfill and our lives are not intended to be spent questioning our existence—we are needed. Thanks for giving us an opportunity to be honest. (That's not always easy!)

James Jones Jr., BS, MA
City Church of Goldsboro
Goldsboro, NC

Dedication

This book is dedicated to you the reader because you are so unique and so very special. There's no one like you in the entire world!

Acknowledgments

Landon Schott and the entire Famous Publishing team made this God dream come to life. Landon, thank you for not only being so available and supportive throughout this process, but also for being an encouraging friend.

Justine Hanin is an amazing artist and talent—thanks for making this project look so great.

Jim Kochenburger, Jimmy Stewart, and the editing team, much appreciation for you for your thorough editing skill and meaningful insights. Thanks for keeping me on track!

Mal, you believe in me more than I believe in myself most of the time! Thank you for just being you and sticking with me. #WifeForLife H.B.S.P.

To Mallory's and my amazingly supportive parents—you have given to us and done for us things we don't deserve, that people wouldn't believe, and that the world would be so jealous if it knew it all. We love you so much!

To Pastor Steve and Sharon Holder, I cannot express sufficient gratitude for your faithfulness. Thank you for paving a way, supporting me in ways some people will never even know, cheerleading, and just being my spiritual mom and dad.

Thanks to Pastor Jentezen Franklin, Cherise Franklin, and Free Chapel; Forward Conference is the soil where this book was seeded in my heart!

Daniel and Caitlyn, you have been like no other humans on planet Earth. Thank you both for being such a major and integral part of my development and growth as a person and follower of Jesus. Can't wait for you both to write books and share your life stories!

To Mark and Melinda, you both believed a crazy guy like me could fit into a local church.

To Lu, thank you for simply believing in me like no other person could. There is so much more I could say, but you will hear me say it in person.

Introduction

Thank you, thank you, and thank you! I can't thank you enough for investing in this project. Thank you for not just investing money, but for investing your time to read this. Thank you for investing your heart into this while you journey through this book. Thank you for trusting my voice in your life. It is almost unbelievable to me that you are holding this book in your hands right now. Please know I am praying for you. I pray for your calling and the plans that God has for your life. The plans God has for you are bigger than you might think, and even bigger than you could even dream about! Mal and I love you!

Love always,
Chrétien

Table of Contents

Falling Star

*"I wish everyone could get rich and famous and have
everything they ever dreamed of so they would know
that's not the answer."*

— Jim Carrey

It's a typical winter evening in eastern North Carolina. The
sun has just set over the expansive tobacco fields that line the
two-lane country roads. Christmas is only five days away,
and there is still so much work to do to ready our local church
and youth ministry for the celebrations. With everything
going on—from shopping, family time, eating (of course!),
preaching, wrapping gifts, and leading teams—you better
believe I still find time to scroll and double-tap on some
Instagram!

On this particular night, I found myself on a favorite,
familiar account: Pastor Carl! Pastor Carl is one of my all-time
heroes. He's a preaching machine, has such an evangelistic
gift, travels the globe, has a growing, influential church in a
great city, and is super tall and *uber* buff! Almost all of these
things I listed are traits about Pastor Carl and not me! How
I would love to travel around the world, encouraging others
and preaching good news, and pastor a church in a massive,
creative, "happening" city—and how I would love to be

super tall and megabuff and have an easy name that people can spell and pronounce right!

"God, why couldn't you make me like Pastor Carl?!" I yell to myself with no audible answer from above. The only thing that makes this night different from any other night is that while I'm scrolling and double-tapping every picture on Pastor Carl's Insta—wishing I was tall, buff, and him and not me—I'm driving a tiny pickup truck fifty-five miles per hour down a two-lane country road in dark, eastern North Carolina.

I don't even notice the dump truck stopped in the middle of the road until it's beyond too late. Without hitting the breaks on my pickup or looking up from my cell phone I slam into the back of the dump truck and black out...

Waking up, I orient myself in the very smoky truck cabin. I try to open the driver's side door to get out but realize the road is blocking me in—the truck is lying on the driver's side. I have no way to get out. Panic sets in. There's blood all over my hands. I am hanging in midair, my seat belt holding me in place. As I unhook my seatbelt and stand up, I can hear a man's voice yelling frantically. Standing straight up in the cabin of the truck, I try to open the door or window, anything to get out, but neither budge. I begin to punch the window with a bloody fist—a feeble attempt to break it (I already told y'all I'm not buff).

I can hear neighbors gathering now, someone yelling for a fire extinguisher. I can hear the fire extinguisher being used and shortly after a man yells to me, "Bend down, I'm going to get you out!" I duck just in time as the window shatters from above and glass rains down on my head. I have such a sharp pain in my stomach, but I am shaking so much from pure adrenaline, that the pain doesn't register. I continue my escape attempt and half climb out of the truck while a stranger simultaneously drags me from the top.

I am loaded into an ambulance, and as the doors shut, I take one last look at the twisted ball of smoking metal that was once my truck. Lines of traffic and crowds of people begin making over the scene. The wreckage disappears as we drive off, and on the gurney in the back of that ambulance, I pray silently to myself that no one finds out the *real* cause of the wreck. I can hear my mom saying: "What have I told you about being on your phone and driving!" Would this change the way my soon-to-be wife thought of me? What would my pastors say? What would the students of the youth group, and even their parents, think of such a poor, careless mistake? All because I was stalking someone on Instagram. All because I wished that I was someone else instead of being comfortable in my own skin—how God made me to be. I will talk more about the real struggle and fight of being consumed by social media in chapter three.

I was so worried of what people would think of me after the wreck, guess what I did? *Guess!* Lean in really close…now put your face right in this book so I can tell you what I did…

I *lied*. When asked what happened, for an entire year I lied. I was so ashamed and embarrassed, I told everyone who asked me about my accident that I didn't know what really happened. "I just blacked out," would be my go-to response.

Please don't judge me! Don't think I am a horrible person. I never lie! "But you told a lie!" you may be screaming out loud. Yes, I did tell a lie. But, I am not a liar! I confessed to Mallory, my fiancée at the time, and then I confessed publicly to the youth ministry I led. You may have made some mistakes in your life, but know this: there is forgiveness. God offers us grace when we repent for our actions, make an effort to live headstrong for him, and make good decisions led by the Holy Spirit.

> **"You may have made some mistakes in your life, but know this: there is forgiveness."**

So let's recap: at this part of my story, I'm like a totally dud falling star. I am insecure, sad, and depressed; I want to be someone I'm not; I'm careless; I have totaled my beloved pickup truck; and *now* I'm openly lying to people! I want to take a moment and tell you that the state of your mind and spirit matter. The unseen, untamed, raw thoughts you think; the invisible emotions that take us on crazy, roller-coaster rides internally from time to time — if unchecked and not brought under control through Jesus and the Holy Spirit will manifest in very real, visible ways in your life.

Unwanted Surprises

My hospital stay began with a few hours of emergency room hangs with the family, multiple tests in scary machines that, let me say, seem to be built for tiny people! I am settled into a hospital room for just a few days stay until I can walk around again on my own. Things go as great as they can in a hospital, and day-by-day I recover more and more. After a two-night stay, I can walk on my own; although, it's incredibly painful.

As the hospital staff begins to draw up paperwork for my release, things take a horrible turn for the worse. Out of nowhere, and rapidly, I begin to lose oxygen and have trouble breathing without being on an oxygen tank. Worse is the growing abdominal pain I am having, and I keep drifting in and out of consciousness. The last thing I remember is being wheeled out of the hospital room in the bed to be taken to emergency surgery in an attempt to find out what is going wrong!

Time drags by. Minutes turn to hours. More than two hours later I am returned to the room from surgery and begin to wake up. "What happened?" I ask of family crowded around my hospital bed. Mama repeats over and over again in a worried tone, "They took care of you, baby." What I really want to know is, what happened? My fiancée (now wife) very frankly let me know: "Chrétien, the doctor had to give you a colostomy." The seatbelt that kept me from flying through the windshield and had saved my life the night of my accident also cut my colon in half. I was having trouble breathing because air and excrement, a.k.a. waste, a.k.a. *poo*, was spilling into my body, pushing on my lungs and making it hard to breathe! The doctor took the healthy part of my colon and put it on the outside of my stomach. Passing gas, doing number two — all of that changed for me in an instant. Having a colostomy means having to wear bags on the outside of your stomach to catch the *poo*! If you have a colostomy, you're my *hero*!

I spent a week in the hospital after my surgery and was released to go home with my colostomy. During my stay, I lost a lot of weight, so I was looking skinny and slim and feeling myself because I could fit into medium shirts again. I do want to say, that is a horrible way to lose weight. I'll stick to cardio and Lean Cuisine next time!

Colosto Life

One of the first times I used the bathroom in public after my accident was when my family and I were eating out at a restaurant. Down in the Bible Belt, about the only thing to do for social interaction is to eat and go to church. Everything else is a sin, *especially* dancing—unless it's during a Pentecostal service, and then it's "in the Spirit." Right before we got to the restaurant, I couldn't help it; I had to go to the bathroom! So I go number two in the colostomy bag and decide I will eat dinner and clean it out when we get home. Does anything ever happen like we plan, though? Rarely.

On the way into the restaurant, my colostomy bag from under my shirt catches the door handle. The bag rips off and hits the ground with a muffled plop and number two splatters all over the floor. People are staring at me and at the poop all over my shirt that in no time is running down my pants. I scoop up the bag quickly and—don't judge me—leave very quickly with no explanation to go home and shower. Again, shout out to all my peeps reading who have a colostomy. You the real MVPs!

I lived three months with a colostomy. Some people live a lifetime with them, unable to have their condition reversed. The reversal surgery—another week's stay in the hospital—and recovery (the reversal recovery was more painful than the accident) were excruciatingly painful. Nothing could compare, however, to the feelings of insecurity and comparison that were on the inside of me. Those unseen feelings and emotions literally almost killed me.

Maybe you feel like a falling star. Maybe you are like me: you struggle with comparing yourself to other people. You find yourself coveting others' gifts, talents, and abilities. Perhaps internally you feel as if you don't belong or that the world would be better off without you. Do you feel like maybe you aren't making a difference in life or will never amount to anything? Do you ever think: "If I only were more like (insert name of friend/parent/pastor/pop star/mentor here): ." How about this thought: "If I looked like (insert name of movie star, supermodel, or friend in homeroom here): ." If you think thoughts like those, then this book is for you! I wrote this book for you because you are more than a burned out, falling star! So get ready to face your insecurities head-on. Get ready to grab control of the steering wheel of your life. As you read with me on the pathway to more success (*anotha one*), read the following passage of Scripture and get ready to shine like the star you are!

> *"So — who is like me?*
> *Who holds a candle to me?" says The Holy.*
> *Look at the night skies:*
> *Who do you think made all this?*
> *Who marches this army of stars out each night,*
> *counts them off, calls each by name*
> *— so magnificent! so powerful! —*
> *and never overlooks a single one?*
> **—Isaiah 40:25-26 (MSG)**

Chapter 1 Discussion

1) Who are some people you've compared yourself to or wished you were like? They can be family, rock stars, leaders, friends, or movie icons.

2) What are some traits those people have that you wish you had? Or tell why you wish you were more like them?

3) If you could sit down for coffee or lunch with a person you listed in question number one, who would it be and why?

4) If you could sit down for a meeting with a person you listed in question number one, what would you say to them? (Be completely honest!)

Side of my truck when I hit a dump truck the Friday before Christmas on December 20th, 2013.

A view from the inside of my truck. I would have went through the windshield and died, but my seat belt saved my life- however, it also cut my colon in half!

Front of my pickup truck after I slammed into the back of a dump truck going 55 MPH while looking an Instagram post of Pastor Carl Lentz preaching!

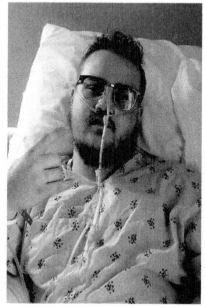

Me in the hospital after my car accident. This is why you don't Instagram and drive. Or compare yourself to others. Weeks in the hospital, a severed colon and surprise colostomy is a horrible way to get over comparison!

A Sky Full of Insecurities

"Wanting to be someone else is a waste of who you are."

–Kurt Cobain

When you look up into the sky at night, you see a beautiful sight! Hundreds of thousands of tiny, white, glimmering stars! A few years ago, a pretty massive hurricane made landfall in North Carolina. Hurricane Irene! While I'm on the subject, can we deviate for just one second and talk about the names of hurricanes? I have so many questions I need answers to.

Why, for example, do hurricanes seem to have normal names? Irene? *Really?* The name Irene makes me think of a rural mother making an apple pie at the kitchen counter as the sun goes down over a wind-blown wheat field. Who really thinks a sweet, gentle name such as Irene is a good name for a crazy-huge, destructive wind and rainstorm?

This is just my opinion, and I'm no expert, but I really think that hurricanes need, like, thug-boss-status names. Let's start naming hurricanes with names like Manic Maniac, Mega-Flex, Fast Trigger, or Trigger Mike. They all seem like tough names that would be suitable for hurricanes. If anyone is wondering, yes, these names came from a Google search of "thug nicknames," and I think they are hardcore and awesome nicknames that are perfect for a storm as epic as a hurricane.

Anyhow, Hurricane Irene ripped through the eastern North Carolina coast one summer a few years ago (I'm back on topic!). One fun thing to do when a hurricane strikes is to go over to your friend's house and have a hurricane party. You and your friends ride out the storm eating and playing board games — two things I love to do! When Irene struck, I was at my friend's house. We rode out the storm, but the night the hurricane passed through we lost power. That may sound like a bummer, but really it wasn't. We were set up for two things: (1) no outside lights on anywhere near us, and (2) a crystal-clear sky.

Samuel Rutherford, a pastor, has said, "After winter comes the summer. After night comes dawn. And after every storm there comes clear, open skies." That isn't just an inspiring quote to keep you in good spirits during trying times. Looking up that night, at the beautiful crystal-clear sky with no outside, man-made light drowning out the view, you could see hundreds of thousands of bright and twinkling stars! It was overwhelming how many you could see; each with a different shape, different twinkle, and unique luster.

Just like no two stars are the same, each of us is unique in the way we are made — and the struggles we face! No doubt, everyone reading this book, in some way in his or her life, can identify with me. You can probably identify with the things I was feeling inside. Maybe you're living your life right now wishing you were someone else. You may find yourself frequently wishing you lived in a different city or state, or maybe even a different country. Most of your time may be spent wishing you could sing or dance like someone else. Do you find yourself wishing you could make people laugh like your friend makes them laugh? Do you wish you could play sports; or maybe you wish you were in a band? Have you ever felt that you got *merked* (a.k.a. "robbed") when it came to looks? You look in the mirror and wish you were skinnier, or perhaps you feel too skinny and wish you had a fuller figure.

I want you to know that if you have big insecurities in your life, God has plans for you that are bigger than your insecurities! Through spending time with him and talking through prayer, and also chewing on his Word, wants to help you overcome your insecurities so that you can help others around you overcome their problems and hang-ups. I will talk more about sharing your life story and what God has done for you later in this book.

> **". . . if you have big insecurities in your life,
> God has plans for you that are bigger than
> your insecurities!"**

Here are just a few of my friends' stories you may identify a little better with. I really love my friends and think they are great, and I love talking about them and what God is doing in their lives! If you are reading this, then (1) *You're my friend* and *you* have a story to tell! And (2) I would love to hear it! Connect with me on social media or visit my website!

Broken Home

One friend I have grew up in a broken home. Her mom and dad divorced when she was in middle school, and her dad moved far away and became detached. During most of high school, she wished she had a normal family. My friend never felt like she was good enough for anyone. She felt like no one liked her, like she was the oddball in the group. My friend had a hard time trusting people and taking them for their word. She became jealous of her friends that had parents who were still married and wished her dad were a part of her life. Eventually she became confused sexually and tried to fill the void with relationships. When that didn't work my friend began to rely heavily on alcohol to numb the unseen, inner pains of life. She made life-altering decisions because of her hurt.

Maybe you wish your parents were still together. Maybe you wish they would talk to you more and that their conversations with you were more open. If you're reading this, I want you to know it's not your fault. You're not responsible for your parents' decisions. Although you may be affected, you're not to blame. Please know that no matter how broken your home or family may be, you belong to a perfect, whole family — God's family! He loves you so much that he sent his best gift, Jesus — his only Son — to be a sacrifice to pay for your sins! He loves you just how you are — insecurities, mess-ups, broken family and all — but he wants to heal you from your brokenness and use you to help put others back together who also come from a broken family ! If you want this wholeness that only God can offer, pray this prayer out loud or to yourself:

God, I am so broken. The family I come from is broken. My heart is broken, and it really affects me and affects how I live each day of my life. I give my heart to you, God, and ask you to heal my brokenness. God, please use me and my story to help those around me who are broken. Holy Spirit, give me the boldness to share the pain of my past and to lead people forward into a life of wholeness in you.

In Jesus' name. Amen.

So if you're serious about living this new resurrection life with Christ, act like it. Pursue the things over which Christ presides. Don't shuffle along, eyes to the ground, absorbed with the things right in front of you. Look up, and be alert to what is going on around Christ — that's where the action is. See things from his perspective.

Your old life is dead. Your new life, which is your real life — even though invisible to spectators — is with Christ in God. He is your life. When Christ (your real life, remember) shows up again on this earth, you'll show up, too — the real you, the glorious you. Meanwhile, be content with obscurity, like Christ.

— **Colossians 3:1-4 (MSG)**

Abuse

Another friend of mine lived in a home where his father physically abused him. When things got stressful, money got tight, or there was a disagreement, my friend's dad would take out his anger on my friend and hit him, throw things at him, and beat him. Millions of young people are physically and emotionally abused each year. You may feel like all you were created to be was someone's punching bag. You could feel like you have no value or purpose in life. Maybe you feel as if you will never get over what was done to you.

I would like you to know that you have a father in God. But he is a good father who wants to bless you, his kid! He has plans for you, and those plans are not to harm you or hurt you; the plans he has for you are good plans. God has big plans for you to succeed in life. God doesn't take out his anger on his children. He doesn't punish you and beat you down. If you have been abused in life, I want you to pray this prayer, if you feel comfortable:

God, I am very hurt. I have been so abused in life. I need your help so that I can be healed from the pain. Thank you for being a good father to me. Thank you for meeting my needs and always being there for me when I need you. Thank you for having a plan for my life, a plan for me to be successful and for me to make it in life. Use me and my story, Holy Spirit, to reach other hurt people and show them the love and healing they can have in God.

In Jesus' name. Amen.

Don't hit back; discover beauty in everyone. If you've got it in you, get along with everybody. Don't insist on getting even; that's not for you to do. "I'll do the judging," says God. *"I'll take care of it."*

—Romans 12:17-19 (MSG)

"God has big plans for you to succeed in life."

Self-Confidence

One friend I have has overcome great self-confidence problems! She went through most of school with bad acne. People would stare at her and even make fun of her. She is such a beautiful young woman, but her acne problem took a very big toll on her self-confidence. She grew so depressed about her looks that she contemplated suicide often. She didn't want to have any friends and found herself wanting to be left alone by the world.

This young woman came into our youth group and chose to follow Christ and live her life for him. God has healed her broken heart and lit such a passionate fire in her! She shares her story with anyone who will listen to her. She is also a gifted leader, leading teams of students and adults in our local church!

God wants to heal your heart right now, too! He doesn't want you to go another day hating yourself. He wants to turn your life around and use you to give other people purpose and make others feel special. If you want this inner peace, pray this prayer to yourself or out loud:

> *God, I ask for your peace to come over me right now. Heal my broken, downtrodden heart. Heal my mind and make me whole. Holy Spirit, I ask for a boldness only you can give — to have godly self-confidence. Use me to help others feel the love you have for them. Let me live my life giving others purpose and adding value to them.*
>
> *In Jesus' name, amen.*

Oh yes, you shaped me first inside, then out;

you formed me in my mother's womb.

I thank you, High God — you're breathtaking!

Body and soul, I am marvelously made!

I worship in adoration — what a creation!

You know me inside and out,

you know every bone in my body;

You know exactly how I was made, bit by bit,

how I was sculpted from nothing into something.

— Psalm 139:13-16 (MSG)

Start a New Chapter

Maybe growing up, you just didn't have any affirmation from anyone. Perhaps nobody believed in the person you were or were becoming. Maybe, like me, you feel you were missing words of affirmation for the talents or abilities you possessed growing up. Now you don't feel special. You don't feel like you have amounted to anything or have anything to offer the world. You may feel like you have more insecurity inside of you than there are stars in the night sky and that you'll never overcome your insecurities and amount to anything in life. Let me tell you right now, there is hope for you! (More to come about that amazingly awesome hope in a few chapters.) Right now, let's start a new chapter in your life! If you're comfortable, why don't you pray this prayer out loud or to yourself quietly:

> *God, I give you these feelings inside of me. The feeling of worthlessness. The feeling of insecurity. The feeling of depression. I give them all to you, God! Holy Spirit, help me to see myself the way you see me. Help me to love myself the way you love me. Help me to believe in myself the way you believe in me. God, I'm saying 'bye to my feelings of insecurities. 'Bye!*
>
> *In Jesus' name. Amen.*
>
> *Your GOD is present among you, a strong Warrior there to save you. Happy to have you back, he'll calm you with his love and delight you with his songs.*

— Zephaniah 3:17 (MSG)

Chapter 2 Discussion

1) What are some insecurities in your life?

2) Have your insecurities hurt you or have they held you back in any way? If so, list a few of the ways.

3) What area(s) of your life have suffered because of your insecurities?

4) List three main reasons you have to overcome your insecurities.

Bye Insecurities

"There are far better things ahead than any we leave behind."

– C. S. Lewis

One thing that I find so very fascinating is watching a balloon full of helium float up to the sky. I don't know what it is about standing on the ground watching a balloon float up to the heavens; maybe it's the mystery of not knowing where the balloon is going. It could be that I love the adventure of it—what cool places will the balloon visit? What cool things will the balloon see? How high will it fly?

What are your thoughts when you see a balloon floating by in the sky? Maybe you feel upset because you can't catch it; you have no control, you can't do anything about it! Perhaps you feel embarrassed because you are the one who accidentally let go of the string? If you're like me, when you gaze up into the vast, blue, endless canvas that is the sky, and you see a tiny balloon racing up to space, you imagine it reaches the troposphere, then the stratosphere, then the mesosphere, then it goes all the way to Mars! If you're wondering for book purposes, I did Google all the layers of the atmosphere to list for you, so don't be overly impressed with me! So maybe the balloon doesn't actually float all the way to Mars, but this is my book; let me dream. Right now I want you to imagine just for a second that the balloon floating away has a list of all your insecurities tied to it. You've just released the string, and all the insecurities you've been holding on to, all the insecurities that have made you depressed and have been holding you back are floating away higher and higher. You'll never catch them now. I want you to get ready to release your insecurities and let them go forever. Release them to float off to space, never to return again!

Don't worry if you're finding yourself stuck in the rut of comparison with all kinds of insecurities, some you didn't even know you had! First, know you're not alone at all! Even some of the most secure people battle with insecurities. Second, know that the world we live in is basically a set-up. It is so incredibly easy to fall into the trap of comparison. All you have to do is open up your phone and get on Instagram, Facebook, or even Twitter. Turn on the TV and flip through a few channels and you can easily begin to feel inadequate with the life you lead, the way you look, the job you work, or the place you live. It seems everywhere you look today there is someone who looks like you want to look, doing something you wished you were doing, on a level that you may not have reached yet. I want to let you know that you need to do whatever it takes to love yourself. More about this later, but if you don't love yourself, then comparison and insecurity will kill your *passion* and *dreams*!

Passion

Passion, or "strong and barely controllable emotion," as defined by Webster, is vital to your everyday life. Passion is what gets you up in the morning. It's what gets you fired up and motivated. Passion is what keeps you going when things seem like they're not working out and you find yourself in dark and trying times. Passion gets you through.

Life without passion is not a full life. I believe life without passion is just merely surviving. But you are a unique work of art created for more than just surviving and being stared at. The *Mona Lisa* is a priceless work of art by famed artist Leonardo da Vinci. As intriguing as Lisa is, viewed by roughly 10 million people every year, it has nothing on you when you live a life filled with passion!

"Life without passion is not a full life."

Insecurities can suck the passion right out of you. When you compare yourself to others, it steals your passion. Anytime you go on social media and get discouraged when you see your favorite singer, speaker, or artist, a little of your passion is sucked away. When you don't celebrate someone else's success and wins in life, you begin to compare yourself. "Why am I not doing what they're doing?" you ask. "Why don't I have what they have?" Eventually, you begin to convince yourself that you'll never "add up" to be what they are. You'll never "make it" like they made it.

Friend, let me tell you, you don't have to add up. You don't have to make it. You are in your own class; you are in a league of your own. You have talents that the people you are looking to don't have! There are gifts inside of you that God didn't place inside of those you look to. Simply put, there are things you can do that they can't.

Please understand how uniquely you were created! Don't let the enemy of comparison steal your passion. Stay passionate about the things God has put in your heart. Keep your strong feelings toward the injustices you want to make right in the world. Let the fire of almost uncontrollable emotion that you feel toward certain things burn so brightly that it burns away your insecurities.

Try giving yourself a pep talk! Motivate yourself! Preach to yourself. When you feel down and that you will never "make it" like Pastor Instagram So-and-So, tell yourself, "I'm special." When you feel your passion slipping and you find you're not on fire like you used to be, motivate yourself! Tell yourself: "I can do this…I will do this!" Promise me, and more importantly, promise yourself, that you will do whatever it takes to get your passion back. Make a promise that you will keep the fires of your passion burning so brightly that no insecurity, setback, failure, or mess-up will ever put it out.

Why do I ask you to do this? Because you will need those strong, barely controllable emotions to reach your dream; you can't afford to lose your passion. You need the passion to make it to your destination. Without passion, you'll quit too early. If you have no passion, you'll never make it through the hard, challenging times of life.

> **"If you have no passion, you'll never make it through the hard, challenging times of life."**

When I think of you and your passions, the story that won't leave my mind is Jesus' passion for you. Here is a man who knew He had to do something hard in life. Jesus knew his end goal. His mission in life was to ransom you from sin's grip. Jesus knew He was to be the payment for your sins so you could live a full life, reconciled with God and secure about your eternity with him.

It's interesting to note that all but one of the Gospel accounts tell how Jesus prayed for God to remove his calling.

Maybe you and Jesus have more in common than you think? Jesus didn't want to do what he was called to do! Maybe you find yourself discouraged in your ministry. You don't like the church you're part of. You and your senior pastor or other church members don't see eye to eye. Maybe God has called you to adopt or foster children and you find yourself so tangled in red tape and emotions that you've asked God to move you or change your calling.

Do you wish you were at that school or church you see on Instagram instead of the one God's called you to? Perhaps you wish you dressed like your Facebook friend or that you were more like the lead singer of your favorite band. Maybe you are neglecting your calling to be a doctor or go into business because you don't feel qualified. Be encouraged! Even Jesus had doubts about what He was called to do.

I believe Jesus offers a powerful secret we can use to destroy the passion-stealers in our lives. Jesus prayed, "Father, not my will, but your will." Jesus understood his life was not his own. He had a mission and a calling to fulfill! Despite the doubts and feelings He may have felt in his life, Jesus prayed for God's will to be done over his feelings, doubts, and insecurities! Soon after Jesus prayed that, he was arrested, beaten, made fun of, and crucified for me and you. Why? Because He chose to step into his calling when he prayed, "Not what I want, but what you want, God!" I really think the nails that held Jesus on the cross didn't keep him up on the wooden beams. I think it was his passion for you, me, and all people.

I want to pray for you about the passions that you have or once had. If you have lost your passions, or maybe you don't even know what they are, I want to encourage you to think, pray, and write a list of things that you are passionate about! Consider praying this prayer privately to yourself or out loud—or maybe you need to scream it at the top of your lungs at this point in your life:

God, I pray for the passions you put inside of us! I ask you to renew and make strong again the passions in our hearts. God, let us not get caught up in doubt or comparing ourselves to other people. Put the passion inside of us, God, to daily walk out the calling you have put on our lives, in the places you have called us to be. God, I repent for not being so passionate about you and the work you've asked me to do. I ask for your forgiveness for being complacent. I ask you, Holy Spirit, to build up my faith and help me to believe I can do the things God has asked me to do. Keep my passion fresh and burning bright for you, your causes, and your will for my life.

In the passionate name of Jesus. Amen.

Dreams

Are you a dreamer? Do you find yourself dreaming a lot? Maybe you consider yourself a realist. You are all about facts and things you can see; you want to get stuff done and see results! Chances are, however, that you categorize yourself; you have at least one dream or another in your heart. I'm not talking about the dreams that you have at night while you sleep, although you very well may dream up these types of dreams while you sleep. The dreams I want to talk to you about are the ones that you contemplate doing, the things you think about accomplishing all the time, the places you want to go.

Famed British diplomat T. E. Lawrence—let me pause here and insert this: who doesn't love British people? We Americans love our British cousins across the pond for many reasons, the main one being their accents! I mean, come on,

Brits have their own royal family. They have a queen. One personal thing I love about the British is their sense of humor. They have mastered the art of dry comedy and humor. Anyhow, T. E. Lawrence has a quote I love. He says, "All men dream, but not equally."

Maybe you dream big dreams that to some people may seem impossible. Perhaps you dream dreams that are relatively achievable and reachable. Maybe you don't dream at all right now. Your dreams may be nonexistent, or the thrill of dreaming has been sucked out of you by a broken relationship or harsh words that you can't get out of your head. If you have convinced yourself to give up on your dreams because you'll never be like "them," rebuke yourself! Don't think thoughts like that about yourself. Don't take that from yourself! Not only will comparison and insecurities steal your passion, they also can be dream stealers. Here are some very wise words come from Proverbs about having dreams and vision for your life: *"If people can't see what God is doing, they stumble all over themselves; But when they attend to what he reveals, they are most blessed"* **(Proverbs 29:18, MSG).**

Don't fall into the trap of comparing yourself to other people's ministries, lives, jobs, and callings or even the homes and cities they live in! When you fix your eyes on other people and the spaces and positions they occupy, you begin to lose a grasp on what God is doing in your own heart, in your workplace, and in your ministry. Your life will deteriorate when you focus on what others are doing, or how they look. You will lose your passion for life, and then you will quit dreaming. You will quit looking forward to the future. Soon you will find yourself in a dark place, where you doubt and question the future. The plans you once made that sounded like a stable way to go, become muddled by the voice of doubt inside your head. The path that you dreamed and charted for your life at one time that seemed like a clear, robust journey to travel on now becomes a challenge, all because you allowed the seeds of comparison to take root and grow.

> **"Don't fall into the trap of comparing yourself to other people's ministries, lives, jobs, and callings or even the homes and cities they live in!"**

No, friend! I want you to dream again! I want you to make plans again. Ask God what He would have you do with your life. Seek his plans for you. Shift your focus from what others are doing—the space they occupy—how their business is growing and their efforts are being blessed. Block it out! Block it out! Block it out! You are most blessed and pleasing God when you focus on the work He's called *you* to do. I really believe you open the door to supernatural blessings and favor from God when you live your live as the person he called you to be, cultivating the garden of dreams He's planted in your heart, and build the life he called *only you* to build.

How special! Think of how much better off your family will be, how better off your work, leadership, church, and community will be when you shift the energy you use comparing yourself to others and focus it on bettering yourself and living your life to the fullest. Don't get discouraged if your dreams don't come to pass fast enough.

One biblical character I like named Joseph was a dreamer just like you and me. Joseph even knew he would be a great, respected man one day. He always held on to his dream and would even share his dreams with his family. I really think the demon of comparison is all in Joseph's story, even though the Bible doesn't outright say it is. When Joseph told his family his dreams of the awesome plans God had for his life, his brothers hated him for it. Joseph's brothers despised whom Joseph was. I think they wanted to be like him! I really believe if someone hates on you and the dreams you have, it really means they want to be like you.

> **"Think of how much better off your family will be, how better off your work, leadership, church, and community will be when you shift the energy you use comparing yourself to others and focus it on bettering yourself and living your life to the fullest."**

Joseph's brothers wanted to kill him but couldn't bring themselves to do it, so instead they sold Joseph into slavery because they were so jealous of him. What a different story we would read if Joseph's brothers from Genesis 37 focused on the calling God had for their lives and the plans He had for them. Maybe we would read a lot more about Joseph's brothers if they dared not to compare and were satisfied with how they were made and the gifts inside of them. What if they would have celebrated Joseph and the dreams he had instead of being jealous of him and hating the calling God put on his life? These are just questions I ask myself.

Do you find yourself celebrating the success of others? How about all those people on social media you see doing "awesome things"? Instead of being jealous and thinking: "That will never be me. Who am I kidding?" try having an attitude of celebration. Give God a "thank you" when you see others succeeding and reaching their dreams.

What I find very interesting through Joseph's story is that even while in slavery, Joseph never stopped dreaming. You can't stop dreaming either! When life throws you a curve ball, and things are not turning out the way you pictured, keep your dream on the forefront of your mind. Maybe you find yourself in a not-so-ideal situation: maybe a broken home or a failing school, or maybe you're without a job. Are you in a "winter season" of life where everything seems dead, dark, and hopeless? Whatever the case, be like Joseph. No matter what you're facing, keep dreaming! Keep having hope. Keep the vision alive! Focus on what God has called you to do and the dreams he put in your heart. Because Joseph focused on the plans God had for his life and kept dreaming, he eventually saw his dreams come to pass. You will too! Dream again, friend. Focus on you and the things that make you unique. Stay close to Jesus. In the words of the great theologian Steven Victor Tallarico: *"Dream on, dream on, dream on, dream on 'til your dreams come true!"*

> **"In the words of the great theologian Steven Victor Tallarico: *"Dream on, dream on, dream on, dream on 'til your dreams come true!"""***

If you're comfortable, pray this prayer to yourself or aloud. I am praying it over your life, but I want you to pray it too!

God, I pray that dreams will be dreamed again! Holy Spirit, help shift the focus from others to me. Help me celebrate the success and dreams of others. Help me have vision for the future again and to be hopeful! God, I ask you help me not to fall into the trap of comparison but instead to work hard at being the person you called me to be, doing the things you've called me to do! I will try my hardest to think positively, keep my head up, stay close to you, and keep dreaming!

In Jesus' name. Amen!

Chapter 3 Discussion

1) On a scale from 0 to 10, with zero being not passionate at all and 10 being very passionate, what's your passion level for life right now?

2) How could you increase your passion?

3) Write down two of the things you dream about most.

4) Is there one thing you think about doing all the time— when you wake up, while you're at work, before you go to sleep at night? If so, what is it?

Love Yourself

"Have you loved you today?"

One of the hottest songs out right now is "Love Yourself" by Justin Bieber from his late 2015 album *Purpose*. Don't be ashamed if you just screamed out loud in delight like a fan girl when you read Justin's name. His hit "Love Yourself" spent 24 weeks on music charts, so if you've listened to just about any radio station for three minutes, you've probably heard of it. If you haven't heard anything about this song, I'll fill you in. It's about an ex-girlfriend who uses Justin's "status" to get into certain places and get special treatment and then dumps him. "Biebs" sings this catchy song telling her how she's not really that special and tells her to go "love yourself!"

I wonder how many of you skipped this intro because you already knew the song, what it's about, and every single lyric and key change to it. Don't read ahead; stay with me because I think Justin is really onto something. What would — not just relationships with other humans — but what would the world be like if we all just genuinely loved ourselves and who we were made to be? Think of some things you don't like about yourself. Feel free to write them down in the margins of this book while I share this story with you from my life.

I never really liked myself! I was never "popular" or "cool" in school. As a matter of fact, back when I attended

Charles E. Bennett Elementary School in the beautiful, small town of Green Cove Spring, Florida, I remember wanting to be so cool and the center of attention. I had a major problem though. For most of elementary school, my mom dressed me. No offense to you, Mom, if you're reading this. I really do love you, Mama. Listen, it's not that my mom had horrible fashion sense. One big factor working against me was that my mom dressed me during the '90s! The era of Jenco and FUBU. Speaking of FUBU, I love Daymond John. He is amazing on *Shark Tank*, a hit show on ABC that I love to watch. He's a great investor, and I think he is a super-brilliant guy, especially for his ideas on the power found in being broke and how "broke" has the power to drive your dreams! Daymond has a book titled *The Power of Broke*. You may like it.

So my mom dressed me in elementary school — and, no, she didn't dress me in FUBU. It was the '90s, so I remember a lot of khaki pants and polo shirts — two articles of clothing I don't like very much today. Give me a scoop-neck shirt, a pair of Chelsea boots, and a leather jacket, and I will *rock it!*

One horrible memory I am about to share with you, I can't get out of my head. I will never forget it. While at school one day, during library reading time, I joined all the other students on the riser steps in the corner where we all sat while Mrs. Rose, our friendly librarian, read a book to us. On this day, however (and I'm not blaming my mom), for some reason I had my polo shirt tucked into my tan khaki pants. However, I am not sure how normal kids tuck their shirts in nowadays, but '90s Chrétien tucked his shirt not just into his pants, but also into his underwear. As I was leaning forward during reading time, so I could hear Mrs. Rose's soft voice read Eric Carle's literary classic, *The Very Hungry Caterpillar*, all the kids in class saw my underwear. Not just my underwear; they also saw my shirt tucked into my underwear. Story time was ruined, and I was devastated.

As the boys laughed and made fun, the girls all had funny looks on their faces, especially Brittany. Brittany was my super crush in elementary school—you know you all have one—and she wanted to know why in the world would I tuck my shirt into my underwear. I hope you're not laughing as you read this. I am confiding in you and opening to you my deepest, most hidden memories! This is no time for laughs.

Needless to say, Brittany and I never dated, and I never—and I mean never, ever, ever—tucked my shirt into my underwear again. From that moment own, I always paid careful attention to the things I wore and how I dressed, and how I carried myself. I always wanted to make a memorable first impression so that people would like me. The problem is, I never really loved me. I didn't love how I looked or how I talked. I despised almost everything about me. I was always wishing I was like that guy who played football, or the famous actor with all the nice cars and sunglasses, or the '80s rock legend with beautiful long hair, or—since I had recently started following Jesus—other pastors who were doing "bigger and better things" that I was.

You know what? For the longest time I didn't even like my own name. Chrétien. Every year in school I would have to explain what my name meant, why it was spelled the way it was, and how to correctly pronounce it. If I was lucky, the teacher was nice enough to call me by my actual name and not make up a nickname—or just yell, "*Hey, kid!*"

I have always been self-conscious about my weight too. I am not the lightest dude in the lunch line, but you better believe I am still going to be in that lunch line. I love food. All types of food! Mexican, Chinese, Italian—and my most favorite cuisine, chocolate cake. I love them all! I don't discriminate against people or food. So, needless to say, I'm a little big, and that affected how I saw myself when I looked in the mirror.

My senior year of high school, I attended an exclusive public high school called Douglas Anderson School of the Arts. I was required to audition in order to be accepted into the school. I was a vocal major and had studied classical voice for six years. I always wanted to be an opera singer because I love music almost as much as I love food. But that is for another book.

While I was attending high school in beautiful Jacksonville, Florida—in the middle of a vibrant, thriving, busy city—my mom and the rest of my family moved to Goldsboro, North Carolina. Right smack dab in the middle of eastern North Carolina. The land of pork skins (which are amazing), chicken pastry (like dumplings but thinner and slimier), Cheerwine, and red hot dogs! If you're reading this and you've never heard of Goldsboro, North Carolina, you're not alone! It's a great city about an hour east of Raleigh, the capital of North Carolina. At my mom's orders, I had to move to Goldsboro with her when I graduated from high school. So on June 1, 2009, I walked across the stage to receive my high school diploma. On June 2, my mom and I made the eight-hour drive to Goldsboro from Jacksonville with everything I owned, and we didn't talk much at all.

When I first moved to Goldsboro, from the big city of Jacksonville, guess what? I hated it! I didn't like where I was, I didn't like the town, I didn't like the weather. Why, of all places, did I have to move to Goldsboro? I asked God that almost every day of my life for the longest time. So, here I am: I am still very young in life and I hate how I look, I hate where I'm living, and I even despise my own name. Sounds pretty hopeless, huh? Let me tell you if you're reading this, even if you find yourself facing those same feelings, even if you find it hard to love yourself, I am telling you: there is hope!

One thing I realized, and you have to realize this right now before we go any further, you need to stop staring in the mirror at yourself, trying to fix what is not broken. Quit looking into the mirror with a frown of disgust, hating every bit of you staring back. Today is a new day. Today is the day you start loving yourself!

Another thing you must learn to do is to talk to yourself the right way. Quit talking down about yourself, to yourself. Quit saying that you're stupid or ugly. Don't walk around saying you'll never amount to anything. Start preaching positively to yourself. Wake up and ask yourself, "How can I work toward my dreams and calling today?" Speak life to yourself, not death. Repeat to yourself what God already says about you. Post these scriptures on your mirror and read them to yourself every morning when you start your day. And before you lay your head on your pillow at night, remind yourself of them!

$\qquad$ **"Start preaching positively to yourself."** $\qquad$

Body and soul, I am marvelously made!
— **Psalm 139:14 (MSG)**

[I am created in] Christ Jesus to join him in the work he does, the good work he has gotten ready for [me] to do, work [I] had better be doing.
— **Ephesians 2:10 (MSG)**

35

God is God....He made [me]; [I] didn't make him. [I am part of] his people, his well-tended sheep.
— Psalm 100:3 (MSG)

Jesus broke down the entire Bible and made it super simple for you and me to follow. Jesus basically said, "Listen, if you do choose to follow Me, all you gotta do is these two things; let Me make it real easy for you": " *'So love the Lord God with all your passion and prayer and intelligence and energy.' And here is the second: 'Love others as well as you love yourself.' There is no other commandment that ranks with these"* (**Mark 12:29-31, MSG**). Jesus said, "Love God and love people" — that's all you have to do. But not just "love" God, but "love him with all you've got."

The second rule Jesus gave us was to love people. But not just a simple "love others." Jesus said for us to love others the way we love ourselves. I have a question for you. Have you thought about how you're going to love others if you don't even love yourself? How can you add value to others if you don't see yourself as valuable? The bottom line is, in fact, it's impossible to love others if you don't love yourself. You just simply cannot do it.

That's why you need to repeat what God says about you, honey! Dude, when you feel so inadequate and beat up by the devil of comparison — when you hear, "You'll never do that," or, "You'll never make it there," or, "You will fail," then treat Satan like the punk he is. Treat him like Jesus treated him. Repeat what God says about you and who you are! Every time Jesus was tempted and tested in the wilderness by the devil in Matthew 4, he simply repeated what God had already said about him!

Begin today to change the way you see yourself. When you feel your insecurities rise up, or when you begin to compare yourself to other people, or when you doubt yourself or you don't like the way you look, memorize the short scriptures just mentioned and repeat what God has already said about you. Shift the way you talk to yourself. Change the language you use to describe yourself. Learn to repeat what God has already said about you and the life you live and what you are called to.

> **"Begin today to change the way you see yourself."**

And if you think that I'm going to stop praying for you and believing in you; honey, you should go and *love yourself* (yes, I sang that to the tune of the "Biebs'" song.)

You can pray this prayer if you want, but I want to use it to pray for *you*!

Holy Spirit, I ask that you begin to shift something on the inside right now. I pray for minds to be altered and changed. I pray hate and disgust are no longer felt when the mirror is looked into. Replace sadness with gladness for who you created us to be. Help us, God, to love ourselves and see ourselves the way you see us and love us: as wonderful and magnificent; as talented, smart, creative, and unique. Help us to love ourselves so that we can love other people and bring light and hope to the dark world around us.

In Jesus' name. Amen!

Chapter 4 Discussion

1) Have you ever tucked your shirt into your underwear? If you answer yes, please take my advice and never do it again.

2) Do you find that you think mostly positive thoughts, or do you tend to think mostly negatively?

3) If you answered mostly negatively, what can you do to think positive thoughts more often?

4) Make a list of at least ten things that you love about yourself.

U B U

"Be a Fruit Loop in a world full of Cheerios."

I love space! I remember in grade school taking part in a weeklong celebration called Space Week. Sounds epic doesn't it? Unlike the underwear-shirt-tucking incident, this is actually a great memory from grade school.

At the beginning of Space Week, we would spend the entire morning cleaning out the classroom. We would push all the desks up against the wall and make a great big empty space. Then we would piece black tarp together and make a giant bubble. Our super-creative teacher would attach a fan to one end of the bubble and turn it on, inflating the giant black tarp. The bubble would be so big, you could stand up on the inside of it, but it would be super dark except for the really cool backlights inside — forgot to mention those.

For the rest of Space Week, as a class we would design and build planets, stars, rocket ships, satellites, and more and hang them in the space bubble to make a giant model of space! It was amazing to get in that tent and see our solar system laid out in specific order, with no two planets or stars the same. Each planet was different and beautiful in its own right: Saturn with its cool rings, Jupiter's gorgeous red blotch. Neptune has a pretty royal-blue color and an Earth-swallowing storm blotch — a stark contrast to tiny Mercury, small and hot, close to the Sun. As unique as all the plants are, each one's size and location in the solar system helps to maintain the balance of the entire system and life on Earth. Removing just one planet out of alignment would catastrophically affect the whole system!

You're like a planet; did you know that? You are so unique. You have traits that no other human on Earth has — and there are roughly 7 billion humans here on this planet. Just out of curiosity, if you could be one planet in our solar system, which one would you be? You can't say the one that starts with a *U* either because that is inappropriate and a lot of immature people would laugh.

I would probably be Pluto. Why Pluto? Because Pluto is the smallest planet, and I am usually the smallest guy in the room. Pluto isn't even a planet anymore, you say? OK, well, when I was growing up, I was taught Pluto was a planet, and just because some mean NASA guys decided in 2005 they didn't want Pluto to be a planet anymore doesn't mean it's not a planet in my book. Tiny things need love too. Just a note, for all educational purposes, I have to write that as of 2005 Pluto was, in fact, no longer classified as a planet but as a dwarf planet.

What are some of the talents you have? Do you play an instrument? Write poetry? Are you schooled and well-versed in constitutional law? Perhaps you're like my friend Carrie who is a dental hygienist. She uses just what's in her hand to make a difference in people's lives. While she is putting sharp instruments and hook-like things in people's mouths and cleaning their teeth, she encourages them, lifts them up, and adds value to them. Maybe you like to communicate with people; perhaps you're an organized, efficient manager. You shouldn't have to think long to come up with at least a few things you're good at.

My father-in-law is one of the most gifted and kindest doctors in our area, and he uses his position as a platform to help others. My friend Caitlyn is one of the most amazing stay-at-home, home-schooling moms ever! Her kids are super smart and respectful. You have to understand that there's no one else like you in the world! *Wow!* You're the only one. There are things that only you can do. What if you didn't do those things, though? What if you gave in to the negative thoughts? What if you just succumbed to comparison and let your insecurities grow up like weeds and choke the life out of you?

You have to be you! Or, U B U! Three simple letters that have life-altering effects.

When you wake up and get going with your day, U B U. At work, U B U. Out to lunch, U B U. Got a big interview, U B U! I think you get it! You have to be you because no one else can or ever will.

Moses is like a biblical hero. Moses is to the Bible what Obi-Wan Kenobi is to *Star Wars.* Just like Obi-Wan brought stability, legacy, and strength to the Force, Moses brought stability, legacy, and strength to God's people—the Hebrew people in the Old Testament. If you have never heard the story, the Hebrew people were slaves to the Egyptians, working really hard for them and suffering from treacherous living conditions and ill treatment. God wanted to save his people and he asked Moses to step up and do it. Unlike Obi-Wan though, who carried a mega-cool light saber, Moses had only a stick.

But before I tell you how Moses became like a rock star of the Old Testament, did you know Moses was self-conscious, probably just like you are? I love getting a glimpse into his life; it makes me feel so human and "normal." Moses was so worried about the way he talked. He had a little stuttering problem, a speech handicap. He was so doubtful when God began to talk to him about leading the Hebrews to freedom. Moses was worried that people wouldn't trust him. He didn't think people would listen to him. He didn't even believe that people would believe in the vision he had or that he had even heard from God!

Moses even asked God if his older brother, Aaron, could be the chosen one. Have you ever told God something like that? "Just let them do it, God. I'll never do that." "What will people think of me? They'll judge me, I can't do that." "They're way cooler." "She's way more confident." "He is skinnier and has more hair." We are more like the hero Moses than we think! When you are not comfortable being you, you miss out on the plans God has for you. And that applies to all of us.

Anyway, Moses didn't have a cool light saber. But he did have a "staff" — a stick thingy like a branch. And in Genesis 4, God asked Moses what he had in his hand. Of course, it was a typical shepherding staff, a tool of the trade back then. But this was a special staff because it was Moses'. There was no other staff like it. Years after Moses died, his staff was coveted, and just as unique as when he used it himself.

So God asked a scared, insecure Moses what was in his hand and then God asked Moses to throw it on the ground. Moses, of course, did what any of us would do if we heard the audible voice of God speaking to us through a bush that was on fire but wasn't burning. He dropped the stick like it was hot! When he did, it turned into a snake. Again, like any of us would have done, Moses ran!

When U B U, it unlocks the supernatural power of God in your life. The miraculous, unexplainable begins to happen when U B U. This event in Moses' life, when he stepped up and used what was in his hand, set into motion Moses' destiny. With that staff, Moses would part the Red Sea. The staff would be used to turn the Nile River into blood and make frogs come out of it to plague Egypt. Moses would even use the staff to perform miracles that would sustain and help all throughout the Hebrews' time in the desert wilderness.

> **"When U B U, it unlocks the supernatural power of God in your life."**

Stop for a second though, if you can, and just think: what if Moses had not done what God asked him to do? What if he had never gotten out of the trap of comparison or let go of his insecurities? The entire Bible would not be written as it was; history and destiny would be reshaped. I know you're interested in Moses' life story, but please listen to me: *you* have to do the things God has called *you* to do. You have to step up to the plate. You have to use *your* talents, gifts, abilities, personality traits, wealth, time — whatever you have in your hand — to accomplish your God given destiny. U B U. Dream the dreams you have. Set goals. Be a good steward of your resources and your gifts.

Just like the Hebrews needed Moses to step into his purpose and be who God called him to be, there are people who need you to be secure in whom you are in Christ and not be fearful. U B U. Just like the balance of the solar system hangs on each planet, so the balance of your family, community, and sphere of influence hangs on you being you. You can do it. Take some time to write, maybe in the margins of this page, some things you are good at, some talents and abilities you have or your personality type. Think of things you want to do and dream of doing and write them down.

I believe when U B U, dreams are going to come to pass. Your destiny is going to be set in motion, and God's supernatural favor is going to be released in your life! While you write your gifts down, let me pray for you; and you can pray this for yourself too if you feel comfortable.

God, I pray right now you would begin to open up eyes so that we might see the uniqueness of who you've created us to be, the different gifts you've given us, the talents you've placed in our lives. God, we want to use what's in our hand to bring about your plans on Earth. Help us, Holy Spirit, to stop comparing ourselves to other people. Help us to be who you've called us to be. Help us to have the fearless confidence that only you can give, Holy Spirit, to do the things you've called us do to. We're excited — and the best is ahead!

In the name of Jesus. Amen!

Chapter 5 Discussion

1) What's your favorite planet in our solar system? Why?

2) Moses had a staff in his hand, but what do you have in yours? What are some talents, abilities, or opportunities you have to make a difference?

3) Make a list of at least ten things that you can do really great and with ease.

4) What do people need or want most when they seek your advice or help?

6

You're a Star

"Everyone's a star and deserves the right to twinkle."

–Marilyn Monroe

How high can you count? Like, what is the highest number you can count to by yourself? Have you ever just started counting aloud to see how high you can get? Ever heard of Jeremy Harper? He's from Birmingham, Alabama. He gained fame for being in the *Guinness Book of World Records* for counting to 1 million. Jeremy started counting on June 18, 2007, and he didn't leave his house or shave until he got to 1 million. On September 14, 2007—almost three months to the date from when he started counting—he finished, securing his title as the world-record holder for counting to 1 million. What a feat. That's a lot of numbers.

As crazy as it sounds, though, there's something I've got to tell you that's crazier. Do you know how many stars there are? Scientists believe— their absolute best guess—is there are over 40 sextillion stars in existence. That's forty with twenty-one zeros. More than 40,000,000,000,000,000,000,000 exist. Isaiah 45 really helped me to learn to be content with who I am and who God made me to be. It is beautifully written in The Message version of the Bible:

"So — who is like me?
Who holds a candle to me?" says The Holy.

45

Look at the night skies:
Who do you think made all this?
Who marches this army of stars out each night,
counts them off, calls each by name
— so magnificent! so powerful! —
and never overlooks a single one?
— Isaiah 40:25-26 (MSG)

God marches the army of stars out each night, all 40 sextillion of them. The Bible says he counts them off and calls them each by name. Let's just use human Jeremy Harper's method of counting and do some math. If you were to count each star as awesome, powerful, omnipotent God does, and you counted like human Jeremy from Alabama does, it would take you 5 quadrillion, 699 trillion, 426 billion, 495 million, 208,000, and 919 hours (5,699,426,495,208,919) to count them all. That's 237 trillion, 476 billion, 103 million, 967,000, and thirty-eight days (237,476,103,967,038) to count all the stars. Still with me? If you were to count all the stars in existence and not lose count, you would count for 33 trillion, 925 billion, 157 million, 709,000, 576 weeks (33,925,157,709,576). Not that you could ever dream of living this long but, if you counted all the stars, it would take you 652 billion, 406 million, 879,000, and thirty years (652,406,879,030).

God counts the stars each and every night! How mind blowing is that? He marches each one out into the sky. It's seems nearly impossible! Modern-day geologists (scientists who study the Earth) believe that our planet is only 4.5 billion years old (evangelical scientists believe the earth is about 10,000 years old). Either way you believe, you could have started counting the stars as soon as the Earth was formed and you would be nowhere near finished counting the stars in the sky. God does this every night! #MindBlown yet?

Not only that, Isaiah records that God calls them each by name. So if there are 40 sextillion stars in the sky how could you ever name that many? Webster's Unabridged Dictionary is filled with over 500,000 words. Can you recite that many words? If God recorded the names of each star, which he very well may have, He would have 80 quadrillion (80,000,000,000,000,000) books the size of Webster's Unabridged Dictionary filled with the names of each of the stars. That means there are words and names that God speaks and uses that we've never even heard of.

This hurts my brain! I wonder what some of the names or words sound like? More than that, I wonder where he would keep all those books with the names in them? Like, is the Grand Canyon God's library of books with star names? Maybe God keeps his star-name books in Area 51? I'm no conspiracy theorist, though.

Why did I just go through all this trouble to hopefully not bore you with these numbers but help you understand what a feat it is to count stars and name them? (And to tell you that God does it every time the sun goes down?) Because I want you to see if God cares for each star so much that he counts them and names them, how much more does He care for you? Do you believe that?

Sure, God created every living thing: trees, animals, oceans. But humans are the only creation he physically breathed his breath into. You are so special to God. You're not just another fish in the sea. You have a calling on your life. You are chosen, talented, gifted. You have purpose inside of you waiting to come out. Your family, community, the world all need you to smile, be happy, and start being who

God called you to be and doing what God called you to do. You are so unique! Another verse I love that has really helped me shift my views on myself and who I am in Christ only confirms God's awesome naming power and love for us: *"He counts the stars and assigns each a name. Our Lord is great; with limitless strength. We'll never comprehend what he knows and does. God puts the fallen on their feet again"* **(Psalm 147:4-6, MSG).**

Know that just as God counts the stars, He's counted you. He knows exactly where you're at and what you're going through. He sees you. Don't be caught up on whether man knows your name or not or if people know what you're doing and where you're doing it. God says, "You're counted and accounted for." Just like He gave each of those stars a name, God has named you. I want you to believe again that the God we serve is a great God and has limitless strength to offer you and great plans for your life. The things God has planned for you and the places he wants to take you, you'll never comprehend or understand. You have to trust him. Follow him daily. Listen to the inner tugging, the inner voice of the Holy Spirit. He wants to help you make the right choices, to lead you through the right doors.

> **"Just like He gave each of those stars a name,
> God has named you."**

Maybe you've made some mistakes — you've really blown it a time or two. Don't count yourself out. Don't quit just yet. We serve a God who puts the fallen on their feet again. You still have purpose and value. God still wants to accomplish great things inside you and through you. Surrender your pride and repent and ask for his forgiveness. You may need to apologize to some people for your actions. Be bold and encouraged; you can do hard things. You are so unique. God has counted you and He's putting you back on your feet. He is restoring your spirit, getting you ready to shine like the bright star he made you! The gospel message is that in a sky full of stars, God sees you, counts you in, names you, and thinks you're so special that he gave the best for you. If you feel comfortable, pray this prayer:

> **". . . in a sky full of stars, God sees you, counts you in, names you, and thinks you're so special. . ."**

God, thank you for making me special. Thanks for breathing your breath, your Spirit, into me. Thanks for making me special and unique with a calling and a purpose. I pray for the plans and the purpose you have for my life. Help me step into my calling. Help me to accomplish the things you have for me to do while I'm on Earth. Holy Spirit, lead me and guide me. Help me make daily decisions to follow Jesus and the plans he has for my life.

In the name of Jesus. Amen!

Chapter 6 Discussion

1) Do you like math? If yes, please use the Order of Operations and solve the following equation: 20+3(5-1)=

2) Do you have a hard time believing that God knows you, sees you, and has counted you? Why or why not?

3) If you were God, what are some creative places you would keep all those books with star names in them?

4) What is something you believe God is calling you to do in or with your life?

Shine, Baby, Shine

"Shine bright like a diamond."

–Rihanna

I hope by now the view you have had about yourself has shifted. I hope you see how much you are valued and loved by God. It's my heartfelt prayer that you realize how uniquely you were created, how you're so full of special talents and abilities that no one else has. I hope you see how imperative it is for you to run the race you were called by God to run. Wake up, smell the coffee — or white chocolate mocha for me, personally — and see that you have to stay in your lane and dare not compare yourself to others. Just remember, life's always unfair when you compare! I hopefully have written and convinced you of your worth. Now I want to give you some practical tips on how to shine the brightest you can!

Jesus' own words were:

Here's another way to put it: You're here to be light, bringing out the God-colors in the world. God is not a secret to be kept. We're going public with this, as public as a city on a hill. If I make you light-bearers, you don't think I'm going to hide you under a bucket, do you? I'm putting you on a light stand. Now that I've put you there on a hilltop, on a light stand – shine! Keep open house; be generous with your lives. By opening up to others, you'll prompt people to open up with God, this generous Father in heaven.

—Matthew 5:14-16 (MSG)

Realize that with your talents and abilities Jesus has put you on a hilltop, on a light stand, and He's ready for you to shine! Shining your light, like Jesus said, is all about evangelizing, or telling the good news. *Evangelizing* is just a big word for telling your story.

Your Story

One of the first things you can do is to begin telling your story! This is so easy. Literally anyone can do it, *anyone*. Everyone has a story, and each one is beautiful. No two stories are alike. If you're reading this, you have a story and you need to begin telling it to anyone who will listen: your mom, cousin, youth leader, church, manager, classmates in homeroom, teacher. Everyone needs to hear your story!

> **"Everyone has a story, and each one is beautiful."**

Sometimes telling your story can be stressful, even fearful. I have found that taking time to organize and write out your story beforehand makes it easier for you to tell it to others. Maybe you have a way you like to tell your story. If you have your own way of doing it, that's awesome—get to tellin' it! If not, consider using the simple outline in the next paragraph to help you organize your thoughts. Begin telling your story every chance you get. I want you to get over the thought that evangelizing is difficult and just for "older people" or just for church leaders. Jesus called us all to make disciples, and using this simple abbreviation I have come up with will help you to evangelize:

It's S.M.C. and stands for: **Searching, Meeting, Changing.**

Searching is when you tell what your life was like before you met Jesus. What was your life like when you were searching for the answers and you seemed to be lost? For me, I was so sad. I hated life and where I was at and who I was. I never realized how much Jesus loved me, how unique I was, or the plans he had for my life. I would spend all my mornings sleeping and not get out of bed until lunchtime; I had no job and no ambitions! But one day that all changed. I met Jesus.

The *M* of S.M.C. is for **Meeting**. It's the part of your story when you met Jesus. Tell how you met Jesus and where you met him. What was your first meeting like, and how did you feel? When I was 18 years old, I attended a local youth group on Halloween night. It was a Fear Factor-themed party. There was a cricket-eating contest, and everyone was dressed up in costumes. After the festivities, we hung out really late playing indoor whiffle ball.

As I was driving home that night on October 31, 2009, I remember thinking how nice everyone at that church was and how they welcomed me and made me feel like I was a part and like I belonged. I felt the Holy Spirit tell me that I needed to change; my heart and life needed to change. So I pulled over to the side of the road in my Nissan Xterra with its thick, fake, snow-leopard-fur headliner, and I prayed a quick prayer. I prayed: "Jesus, I know you're real by how these people have loved me and welcomed me. I haven't lived a very good life, but I want to start living for you." After my simple prayer, I finished the drive home and told my parents how great this new church was and the people were. It took them a few months, but eventually my parents agreed to come along with me.

What was your meeting with Jesus like? Have you had that experience yet? If not, Jesus is waiting on you! You have a story to tell. You've been through things. You have experiences to offer to help others get through life. Consider praying this prayer if you want to live for Jesus and serve him with your life, or if you feel like you need to rededicate your life to him and have a fresh start:

> *Jesus, I love you. I know you love me because you died on the cross for me. I accept your love. Thank you for making me so unique. Holy Spirit, help me to live for you and follow you wherever you want to take me.*
>
> *In Jesus' name. Amen!*

If you prayed that prayer, you have just met Jesus! Right here reading this book! Now you have to start telling your story!

The final letter, the letter C of S.M.C., stands for **Changing**. People need to know how Jesus is actively changing your life. Since I've met Jesus, He's changed me a great deal! I no longer sleep until noon. Instead of criticizing others, I try to encourage everyone I meet and smile at them. Instead of living selfishly for myself, I try my best to serve others and help them make it in life. Jesus has also helped me to love myself and love where I am — to be content. He has changed me so that I value myself more and see my own uniqueness. He has helped me to see that I don't need to be jealous or compare myself to others, that my life's better when I don't

do those things. So take some time right now to write your
story out. Use the S.M.C. outline below and write down your
story:

S. <u>Searching</u>

M. <u>Meeting</u>

C. <u>Changing</u>

Safeguard Yourself

One huge thing that has helped me that I think will help you
shine like the supernova star you are is safeguarding yourself
against things you struggle with. This is going to take some
time and prayer on your part. I would even considering
talking to a friend or mentor about what you're going through
and get their advice on ways you can safeguard yourself and
set yourself up for a bright future. For me, I struggled with
comparison. Ways that really helped me safeguard myself
were to turn off all notifications on my iPhone for social
media. Who cares if someone else just "liked" my post on
Instagram? Is it that big a deal if someone left a comment on
one of my pictures on Facebook? Do I really need to know
immediately if someone snapped me on Snapchat?

This not only has saved me a lot of time — I don't check my
notifications every second I get one — but it also has saved me
a lot of heartache. What if no one likes that picture or post?
What if my Snapchat stays dry? I have more things to worry
about in life. I am a bright shining star and I light up the
world with God colors. If you are attached to the phone every

second of the day checking notifications, just go to Settings on your smartphone or tablet and turn off notifications. Maybe you will need to set up accountability software on your smartphone or tablet devices that will help friends hold you accountable. Perhaps a safeguard for you may be having a friend be honest with you when you talk negatively or gossip about someone. Whatever it is, please start the conversations, pray, and evaluate your life. You are too unique and talented to live a life that is not safeguarded. God has plans for your life, but it's your responsibility to be responsible and make the right choices!

Get off Snapchat and Snap to Work!

One big thing for me was that I had to learn to get off Snapchat and snap to work! I had to quit sleeping the day away and go out and get a job. I want to tell you, please dream big. Don't let anyone discourage you from dreaming massive dreams. Please realize, however, that it is going to take very hard and very consistent work to make those dreams come true. I had to pry myself off of Facebook and actually read books. Facebook can't teach you the principles that leadership expert John Maxwell can when you read a few chapters from his books instead of scrolling an unchanging timeline of your friends' food pictures and boyfriend-girlfriend posts.

> **". . . it is going to take very hard and very consistent work to make those dreams come true."**

Develop some self-control. Instead of spending those hours on Facebook, actually read some books or blogs. For me, instead of posting perfect Instagram moments of my entire life, I had to learn to get off of Instagram and *live* my life. Something super practical that really helped me was turning off all notifications on my iPhone for social media apps. Come on, do you really need to know every time someone likes a picture on your Instagram or reacts to your posts on Facebook? That Snap can definitely wait, and you don't need to view it instantly. I have found that I don't waste as much time scrolling and double-tapping away at everyone's lives. I have more time to actually live mine! It's awesome.

I think we should celebrate how God is using others and what He's doing in others' lives around the world. Don't get so caught up in others people's social media lives that you let your life pass you by. Get off Instagram and take someone out to lunch. Write that message you have been putting off. Start the business that you want to start but haven't made time for. Go to the gym and bulk up, instead of looking at all the fitness accounts on Instagram. Here's a side note: the lives you are seeing on Instagram and social media are not full, entire lives. Social media is nothing more than a quick highlight reel of lives and organizations, where only the good, attractive, positive moments are shown. Rarely do you see tragedies, sadness, and defeat on social media accounts. Instead, you see the fun times. The times where things are perfect and go completely right. Don't be fooled by this. Safeguard yourself! Prepare yourself mentally, physically, spiritually to be ready to fight the real battles you are going to face in your life. The unseen is always greater than the seen!

Unseen > Seen

What if I told you that things you can't see are greater than the things you can see with your eyes? It sounds crazy doesn't it? Something that you can't grasp or hold in your hands can be greater than an object or item you can reach out and physically touch. How can that be? Glad you asked! One thing I believe about people is the things that you don't see about them. The unseen things about them are greater than the things you can see about them, like their Instagram profile, Facebook page, Tweets, and Snaps! Men and women are more than the content they post. Don't get so caught up in comparing yourself to the seen because unless you know that person and are friends with them, you have no idea what the unseen them is like!

> **"What if I told you that things you can't see are greater than the things you can see with your eyes?"**

Take for instance a big oak tree. Oak trees are majestic trees. They can grow to be very large trees, some living to be fifty, even a hundred or more years old. Oak trees, I hope you would agree, are very visible, seeable things! You can look at one, pick its acorns, even climb it. As visible and strong as the oak tree is, there is an unseen force that reckons with it. The wind. Have you ever seen the wind? Can you grab the wind and hold it? As big and tall as the oak tree is, the force of the wind that you will never see will blow it down if the conditions are right.

I believe this is a biblical principle too! In the Old Testament of the Bible, there's a story in 2 Kings 6 that is a big eye-opener (no pun intended; you'll see later) that shows the unseen is greater than the seen. To give you the short version, a prophet named Elisha was in trouble and being accused of being a spy for Israel by an enemy kingdom. The evil king sent a great fighting force to capture Elisha. The enemy king went to great lengths, sending an army with horses and chariots. He had some beef with Elisha for sure. Next time you think you have a beef with somebody, like, would they ever send an entire army to come get you?

Well on that morning, Elisha's servant, a young man, woke up and looked out his window. He was scared out of his mind when he saw horses, chariots, and armed, scary, crazy guys surrounding his entire city. What did he do? The servant did what every great servant would do. He warned his master. Still with me? This is a great story! The servant gave Elisha the report: "Yo, Elisha. Like, outside, there's a bunch of armed crazy guys wanting to capture you and kill you and, like, they have us surrounded and, like, outnumbered, yo." Well the Bible doesn't actually use those words, but I'm pretty positive it went down like that. Elisha told his servant: "Don't worry about it. There are more on our side than on their side."

Now I'm sure the young servant really wanted to be positive and believe by faith here, but I can see him looking out the window after hearing Elisha's words and thinking: "This dude don't be seein' what I'm seein'. Like, there're scary horses, scary chariots, and scary men wanting to kill him." As the thought raced through the young servant's mind, Elisha prayed a simple prayer over him: " Oh, God, open his eyes and let him see." I wouldn't think the servant could be more confused, but if I were him, the confusion level would have just gone up about eight notches. He was probably thinking: "What in the world? I'm looking and seeing the entire city surrounded by the enemy, and my dude Elisha just prayed for my eyes to be opened."

I want to pause here and insert that I really think he was called the "young" servant because he wasn't yet mature enough to understand that the unseen is greater than the seen.

As soon as Elisha prayed over him for his eyes to be opened, the young men looked again—and guess what he saw? Yes, the crazy, terrifying army surrounding the city was still there. He saw something else, though. The young servant saw a wonder he had never seen before: the entire mountainside was filled with fiery chariots and horses that were protecting Elisha.

I'm not going to spoil the rest of the story. I'm not into spoiler alerts; you'll have to go read the ending yourself. My point is there were unseen things that were greater than the seen things. The army of angels protecting Elisha was an unstoppable force. No one would ever stand a chance against an army of angels!

I want you to know that the unseen is greater than the seen. People you look up to and follow on social media have areas of their lives that are unseen. You hold them to a standard of what you see with your natural eye. There are things they do on a daily basis that you will never see. They are fighting battles you don't know about, struggling through things you will never understand. Don't put people on pedestals based just on the things you see in them. They are humans just like you and me. The unseen matters more than the seen. Anyone can be seen and can put on a show in the spotlight. Anyone can post daily spiritual quotes on Facebook. Strive to live it out and be authentic. Seek to be the same person in the shadows that you are in the spotlight. Seek to be the same person you are in your Instagram photos!

Learn Who You Are

I really believe for you to be comfortable with yourself, you have to know yourself. You have to know the gifting and the abilities inside of you. How can you love yourself if you don't know who you are? Everyone reading this is completely different in every imaginable way. But really, we're all similar in the fact that we have talents and traits about us that make us special.

As I write this, I am waiting off to the side at a table in an Apple store to be seen for a MacBook repair. The store is crowded with so many different types of people. I see different nationalities, ages, and sexes. Some people are happy and learning, while others appear aggravated and annoyed. As I look around, though, it's a beautiful picture. The sea of different people really adds a touch of uniqueness to the environment. Apple is known for its "style." All the stores are minimalistic: gray walls, floors, and ceilings. Everything seems cold and industrial.

What if we all were like this, everyone looking exactly the same way and doing the exact same thing? How boring a world it would be! In 1 Corinthians 12, the apostle Paul, who was basically a church leader who traveled around helping other people become comfortable with whom God called them to be, writes to the Corinthians and says this: *"Your body has many parts — limbs, organs, cells — but no matter how many parts you can name, you're still one body"* **(1 Corinthians 12:12, MSG).**

You are part of a bigger body, but you have a great role to play. In Ephesians 4, Paul again writes a letter to people in Ephesus to help them understand their roles in the body. Paul was writing and talking about how Jesus gave everyone a gift: *"He handed out gifts of apostle, prophet, evangelist, and pastor-teacher to train Christians in skilled servant work, working within Christ's body"* **(Ephesians 4:11-12, MSG).**

I believe that everyone born has one of these gifts given by God. All humans are made in his image, so it makes sense that we each would have a gift. Whether you use your gift for

God's purposes and glory, though, that's up to individuals. These roles have been misunderstood, and in today's world, all of these gifts have become titles for church leaders. However, they are not titles; they are gifts, and each person has one. Jesus didn't leave positions or offices and titles. He left gifts.

> **"Jesus didn't leave positions or offices/titles. He left gifts."**

These gifts are expressed through whom you were created to be; in other words, your personality. I think for you to be comfortable in who you are, what you do, and where you're going in life, you have to know which one of these gifts you have. Titles, positions, and offices come and go. Gifts make us unique; they make us the stars we are. When you flow in your God-given gift, it will always make room for you wherever you are. You will also be happier, satisfied in life, and able to earn revenue. Let's go over each of them, and I will give you a brief description of each.

Apostle

People with the apostle gift are generally leaders of leaders. These people love to go into an area where there is nothing, or where there is lack, and build something functional that helps people. If you love to create the future, you probably have this gift. You may have the gift of apostle if you are always working on new ideas and ways to do things better. People with the gift of apostleship usually are prominent business leaders—any C-level positions (CCO, CEO, CFO, and so on) missionaries, church starters, and institution leaders, to name a few.

Prophet

This gift brings correction. Usually law-enforcement, correctional officers, and compliance officials—anyone who sees things that are wrong and loves to make them right may have this gift. If you can walk into a space or a business and tell that something is not right aesthetically, or if you enter a place and automatically think of ways to make it better, cooler, or more useful, then you probably have this gift.

Evangelist

The evangelist is the salesman and marketer among the gifts. People with the evangelist's gift are very passionate about specific things and want everyone to know how great their "thing" is. Evangelists tell everyone they can about what they believe in. They *have* to share with others what they believe in. An Evangelist is often a really great salesperson on a job—or someone who is constantly bringing their friends to church!

Pastor

If you classify yourself as the ultimate fixer, then you may have the pastoral gift. People with the gift of a pastor love to take care of people, specifically hurting, broken people. Do you want to fix things that are wrong with others? Do you find yourself always helping down-and-out friends? Do you love sitting and listening to others' problems and giving advice and trying to help restore them or relieve their pain? You may have the gift of a pastor. People with this gift are usually social workers, counselors, doctors, nurses, or caretakers, or they may even serve as church leaders.

Teacher

People with the gift of a teacher always want to "feed" people helpful things and meet a need they have. Whether it's sharing new information or meeting some other kind of need for a person, a teacher can be found enlightening others, teaching them a better or different way to do something or meeting others' needs. Teachers really want to help people learn and grow stronger in life. Teachers typically occupy roles such as schoolteachers, university professors, managers, motivational speakers, and fitness instructors.

There are many more examples than the few I've given here. Keep in mind, I am talking about gifts that were given to each of us, not titles. Jesus didn't give people titles; he gave them gifts. I just wanted to give you a jump-start to finding out who you are and what you are gifted to do. Resources on spiritual gifts can be found all over the Internet. Write down some traits, talents, abilities, and behaviors you notice about yourself and research as much as you can online and from the Bible. Ask a friend or mentor what they see in you and begin to find out who you are and what you're gifted to do. You are so unique. But you'll never go anywhere or get anything by comparing yourself to other people or comparing your gift to others' gifts. Be who you are. The world needs you! Bottom line: do what you are gifted to do. It's the only way you are guaranteed to succeed! *Shine, baby, shine!*

I used to think that success came overnight. I would look on Instagram and see people doing big things and think: "Wow, they blew up quick! How did they become successful so quickly? Something must be wrong with me. It's taking me too long. It's not happening for me quickly enough." I've heard it said that overnight success takes ten years. Even in the Bible, there are thirty years of Jesus' life that are unaccounted for. We have no idea what He was doing during that time. Not a clue. Kind of like when you leave class to go to the bathroom and come back thirty minutes later and you still have to use the bathroom. Like, where were you? What were you doing? Did you even use the bathroom? That's how I lost bathroom privileges when I was in high school. What was Jesus doing during those times? I'd like to think Jesus was doing what we all have to do: day-by-day living and learning, and taking small, gradual steps each day to get to where we want to go.

Three Magic Questions

OK, so these questions aren't magic at all; I just wanted to call them that. These questions are ones you should ask yourself to help you reach your dreams and goals. Your dreams and goals are accomplishable — you do know that, right? You just have to put in the work and ask yourself tough questions. The late, great champion boxer Muhammad Ali said: "I hated every minute of the training, but I said, 'Don't quit. Suffer now and live the rest of your life as a champion.' " Ali knew it was going to take a lot of dedication to get to where he wanted to be in life. Of course, he was a gifted boxer. But he didn't neglect working out and training.

Don't devalue the preparation. Serve where you are. Stay planted. Build meaningful relationships and friendships. Dig in for the long haul, not just for one quick season. Stay dedicated to your training years and you'll live your life as a champion. Asking yourself these questions could help put you on the right track.

The first question you should ask yourself is: **What do you want?** What do you want out of your life, what do you want to do. What's the end goal look like? Take some time in the margins to answer this question: *what do you want?*

The next question you should ask yourself is: **What do you have?** What's in your hand? Just like we talked about earlier with Moses and the staff he had in his hand, what do you have in your hand? What gift do you have? How about your talents, position, finances, relationships? You need to know what you have so you'll know how to use them to get what you want.

The last question ties the first two together. Ask yourself: **How are you going to fill the gap?** What are the things you are going to do or the steps you are going to take to fill the gap between what you want and what you have? This is the key to seeing your dreams come alive and to living in God's will for the unique person you are! You don't have time to compare yourself to others and what they have and what they want. You need to focus on you and how you're going to fill the gap!

Celebrate Success Right, the Only Way

OK, you caught me. This is definitely a rip-off of DJ Khaled's Snapchat stories. Except he's promoting a crazy drink. I'm telling you this is a very important principle to live by. If you want to overcome comparing yourself to others and live a life without insecurities, you have to learn to celebrate the success of others. It's right, and it's the only way!

I am sure you are like me: there have been many times in your life when you have seen your friend or relative get a promotion, blessing, or crazy, random favor poured out over their lives. They just get the hook-up from God! Now if it had happened to you, you would have shouted and danced and been so happy, doing your little swag walk all around the house. But since it didn't happen to you, if you're like me a little, then you find yourself feeling just a little sad that it happened for your friend and not you. You wonder why you weren't chosen for the promotion or the raise. Why didn't you randomly get blessed? Does God even notice you? "Does anyone notice me?" you think!

Does this sound like the pity party you may throw for yourself? A pity party with yourself is always depressing and never turns out fun. And there's never any cake. I love cake. Anyhow, I'm the happiest when I celebrate with others. I find that when I extend congratulations and I am legitimately excited about others getting ahead in life, I am more content and secure with who I am.

> **". . . when I extend congratulations and I am legitimately excited about others getting ahead in life, I am more content and secure with who I am."**

In Genesis 4, we find two brothers in a very dramatic fight. Cain and Abel both bring an offering to God; however, Cain brought produce from his farm and Abel brought a firstborn animal from his farm (choice cuts of meat). I love a good steak. I love a medium-cooked steak, and you know it's good if you don't have to drown it with steak sauce! God found Abel's offering to be a little more different from Cain's. It was more thoughtful in God's eyes. Instead of celebrating with his brother and bringing a different offering, Cain got so upset about this. The Bible says Cain lost his temper and went into a sulk.

Do you do that when you see others doing what you think are "big" things on Instagram and social media? Do you get depressed when other people are moving ahead with their dreams? Don't be like Cain. Don't sulk and lose your temper. Don't think you don't measure up or that you're not as good as other people. No! Celebrate others' successes. When someone gets a promotion, you be the first to offer your congratulations and a handshake. Smile when other people are blessed with surprises. Be more vocal in celebrating others' accomplishments and when they meet their goals. When you see a friend or follower having an awesome day on social media, just smile and say, "That's awesome," or "I'm so happy for them!" I guarantee, you'll be more appreciative. You'll be a lot happier and a lot more at peace with yourself and your accomplishments in life when you stop comparing and, instead, celebrate others!

The Slight Edge

Don't for a minute think that just because you haven't had your "big break" in life yet that you are unsuccessful or not unique, or that "they" are better than you. You see everyone's success on Snapchat and you want to get on the elevator and take it straight to the top with them. What if I told you that the path to success isn't really a breezy elevator ride at all? The "slight edge" philosophy says that to reach your goals and dreams, instead of riding a smooth elevator quickly to the top, you gradually rise to the top a little bit at a time. Think of it as walking up a slightly inclined ramp. Each day, with each good decision, you take gradual steps toward the top of the ramp, little by little, until you reach your goals in life. So, really, if you think you're going to rocket to the top and be successful, think again and prepare yourself to take the stairs!

Really consider your habits. What are you doing daily to get to where you want to be in life? How about weekly? Monthly? Are you mapping out your goals and plans and really following them? You are special and unique, talented even, no doubt; but you're not excused from the slight edge. Don't think for a minute that you can sleep in every day, play video games all summer, eat Zebra Cakes (which I so love) and never work out, then play starter on the football team in the fall. No way. Not going to happen. See, the slight edge is the idea in life that little choices you deem "insignificant" today, at this point in your life, are actually the major keys that unlock the success you're dreaming of.

Take this book you're reading, for example. I wanted you to read it two years ago. You were important enough for me to write it. I dreamed of it almost every day. I wanted to help you. However, I crumpled up the slight edge and threw it in the trash. I never set my writing goals until recently. I never developed a plan to write a book. I never asked to be held accountable. Never did I study or look into what it would take to get a book published. So, for years this idea sat. The book never wrote itself surprisingly. It's amazing to see now, however.

It happened when I planned out my vision and worked daily to make it happen. I'd write a paragraph a day, a chapter here and there. I'd set time aside during my day to spend drafting and editing. The success you're seeking isn't going to come just from your making the right moves and decisions in life, but also from making the right decisions daily. You see?

Most of the time when people tell me what they want to do with their lives I ask them this question: "What are you doing to get there?" See, your visions aren't going to come to pass on their own. Your dreams aren't just going to knock on your door and present themselves to you wrapped up in pretty packaging with a bow. Don't devalue "small things" like showing up to work on time and doing your job well. Success is built by day-to-day consistency, not one-time accomplishments.

Serve well where you are. Encourage people where you are right now. Value others and seek to love them. Put the slight edge philosophy into practice in your life...now! Set goals for what you want to accomplish and work daily to see them finished. Let the dreams drive you. You may not be where you want to be, but work hard where you are, and one day you'll be right where you want to be. Here it is broken down into two simple slight edge points: (1) See the value in the small things (2) Do them daily. With those two steps and your dreams fueling you, you'll be a success in no time! Just not overnight. Pray this prayer if you are comfortable doing so:

> *Jesus, help me not to get discouraged in the daily living. Help me to love, embrace, and do the "small things" well. Help me to serve with passion right where I am and work toward the dreams you've put in my heart. Help me live a life pleasing to you by making good choices daily. I love you!*
>
> *In your name. Amen.*

Stay Planted

I really wanted this chapter to be super practical for you. One thing that really frustrates me in life is when someone convinces me of a principle or truth but never gives me any practical application of how I can act on it. I feel like I'm so full of this truth but don't know how to let it out. I hope I've done a great job convincing you of how unique, beautiful, special, and important you are. One major key I wanted to leave you with was to *stay planted.*

With social media and the Internet today, it's easy to connect with others and see what they're doing and where they're going. Your world suddenly becomes bigger than your city, community, family, job, and local church. One thing you must fight is the desire to chase and run after the next "big thing." I want to encourage you to stay planted where you are for as long as you can be. Don't just use your position or opportunity as a "stepping stone" to a higher position, title, or paycheck.

Make your mind up to plant your mailbox in concrete and stay awhile. Real, deep, meaningful relationships take years and years to build and grow. Don't jump ship to chase another opportunity; be thankful and make the most of the ones you have now. You are where you are geographically for a reason. It's not just random that you are where you are; it's a divine assignment. There are things you are meant to do right where you are! Don't get discouraged.

You have heard the grass is always greener where you water it! If you don't think your circumstances or place looks so green right now, start watering it. Plant, and sow the seeds you want to harvest! Don't dig up your roots, or withdraw your investment too soon just so you can leave! Now, might God call you specifically to move and go somewhere else- to another location? He could! But until he does, make up your mind to stay planted, serve with excellence, and be the best you can be wherever you are!

Chapter 7 Discussion

1) Have you ever shared your testimony? Why and to whom, or why not?

2) Set a goal to share your story with at least two people this week!

3) What piece of advice was the most meaningful to you from this chapter?

4) What do you think your gift is from Ephesians 4?

5) Answer the Three Magic Questions: What do you want? What do you have? How are you going to fill the gap?

6) Do you think the Slight Edge Theory works? Have you had any success from it?

7) Do you struggle with celebrating the success and gain of others? If so, how can you change up your attitude?

8) Do you struggle with staying planted where you are? Why do you think you have a hard time with this?

Better Together

"I can do things you cannot; you can do things I cannot; together we can do great things."

–Mother Teresa

In the last chapter, I shared about how vital your personal gifts are to the world. I hope you see how special you are, how great you are, and how valuable you are to the world. We all are part of one body, Jesus', and there are *many* parts that make up the body. Talking about the human body, it's so particular that it requires there to be many members: toes, fingers, arms—but they all make up the same body. All the different parts are better together. As many stars as there are in the sky, from Earth we can view only eighty-eight different constellations.

The constellation Orion, named after a Greek mythological hunter, is one of the most conspicuous and recognizable constellations in the night sky. It's a very cool-looking constellation. It has the appearance of a man with a bow, out on the hunt. Did you know seven major stars make up this one constellation? Seven unique individual stars make up one visible picture. The largest constellation in the sky is Hydra. Seventeen stars make up the shape of this snake-looking constellation. The smallest constellation on the other hand, the Southern Cross, is made up of only four small stars.

My point is, when you look up and see pictures in the stars it's because multiple unique, individual stars make up a grand, beautiful picture. Friend, as unique, talented, gifted, beautiful, handsome, and creative you are, you are still just one person. I don't think life was meant to be lived lone-ranger style. Life is to be lived with friends, loved ones, teammates, and partners, not alone by yourself. Life is always better when you live it with someone. I've heard it said that life isn't about what you do; it's about whom you do it with.

Sure, individual stars are beautiful all by themselves, but how cool is it to look up into the sky and see beautiful constellations forming unique pictures? You know, seeing one star is great—it's so beautiful! Seeing constellations together is actually useful. Farmers can plan ahead to plant their agriculture not because of just one star but because of the constellations. Constellations, not just individual stars, also helped ships navigate ocean waters and explorers discover new lands. Don't just be satisfied living your life as a beautiful, authentic you. Immerse yourself in a world made up of others.

Build Relationships

The Holy Spirit has so many roles. Jesus called him "The Helper" and "The Comforter." The Holy Spirit can really help you through life and comfort you through tough times. One role of the Holy Spirit, I believe, is to connect people together! In the Bible, in Acts 8:26-39, we find Philip being led by the Holy Spirit to go and stand in the middle of a random, deserted road. Phillip listened to the Helper, and when he got to the road, a chariot carrying a very important person came rolling by. The Holy Spirit told Philip to jump in the man's chariot. So Philip does, and an unexpected relationship is started between these two random people. Philip witnesses to the man and leads him to Christ.

Can I pause here and say the Holy Spirit better be speaking to me on stuff like this because, I don't know about where you live, but in my city if you go jumping into someone else's car uninvited it could very well be be the last random thing you ever do on Earth. Somebody say, "Holy Spirit, *speak!*" You'd better be hearing him clearly lest ye jump in Grandma's Lincoln Town Car and she lights you up with her .38 Special. Grandmas are thugs where I'm from.

What I want you to understand from this story is that connecting with people and meeting people isn't just a "happenstance." It's not just by luck or accident that you are connected or will connect with people you meet or are going to meet in your life. Begin to see relationships as a divine God connection! Some of my greatest friends and encouragers have been from random connections I have made on Facebook, Twitter, and Instagram. Pastor Chris Hill from Denver has been my Twitter pastor for years, and we've never even met in person! The things he has tweeted have helped me to grow as a leader and get through many dark times!

> **"Begin to see relationships as a divine God connection!"**

I want to insert here how special social media is when you use it in the right way. Please let me say, be a good steward of your social media. Make wise, healthy content posts on your Instagram, Twitter, and Facebook accounts. Watch what you like, share, and retweet. Social media can be a make-or-break factor when someone adds you or follows you. It can make you or break you because it shows a window into your soul, you attitude, and your mind!

You're better when you do life with others, and I believe the Holy Spirit is going to connect you with the right people who are going to better you and encourage you and help you to leverage your gift and make the most of your life. Don't compare yourself or your life to the people you see on social media. Don't compare your life to their highlight reel! Be content with who you, the relationships you have with those around you, and the relationships you are going to build with people. Pray this prayer if you feel comfortable with it:

Holy Spirit, help me listen to you. Speak to me. Lead me in the right directions. Connect me with the right people. Help me to have the boldness and fearless confidence to act on what you tell me. Holy Spirit, I also ask that you keep me disconnected from those whom you don't want me connected with. Help me to encourage everyone I meet and deposit value into them.

In Jesus' name. Amen.

Friendship > Networking

No doubt—we're better together. Our relationships form a beautiful picture, like constellations in the night sky. However, one thing that will mess up the picture is confusing networking and friendship. At first glance, friendship and networking appear to be the same thing. With friendship and networking, you are building new relationships and meeting new people. You find with some people that you are probably interested in the same subjects and have a common interest. You hope the relationship keeps going after your initial meeting.

However, there is a very big difference between networking and making friends. Although networking may be a great opportunity to quickly meet other people who are doing what you are doing or want to do, networking is based more on advancing your personal goals than on getting to know others and really developing deep, meaningful relationships with people. Please don't take from this section that I am against networking entirely. Still, you're not going to be able to make lasting friendships at every event, conference, outing, or party you attend.

I believe, however, that you can network by making friends. I think when you put your personal goals and agendas aside and focus on making friends, networking is more effective. Networking makes relationships about our dreams, our goals, and us. Friendship makes relationships about others — and that is so much more beautiful. Don't let your crave for advancement and "getting ahead in life" turn networking into illegitimate friendship. Friendship is greater than networking because friendship is about understanding not advancement. Networking is about meeting people who have similar interests who can "take you places," while friendship is connecting with everyone, even people who are not like you at all, and just being friends; just being there for each other.

"Friendship makes relationships about others . . ."

I'll never forget one of my coolest friends, Manny, followed me on Twitter and direct-messaged me asking for my cell number. We began to text each other, met up for pizza and coffee (two of the greatest things invented), he is a great encourager and friend. Manny is *the man*! But he didn't need me to get ahead in life. I didn't meet with him over coffee to push my plans or agendas. We wanted to understand each other, be there for each other, and be friends. And that's why friendship is better than networking — because networkers *say* things, but friends *do* things! So start making friends today! Put down your agendas, dreams, and plans. In conversations, make it more about the other person instead of all about you. Keep your word to your friends. Come through for them! Do what you say you're going to do!

One of my best friends — James Jones, a.k.a. "The Bishop" — is a ride-or-die friend for me. James is always there when I need him. He always has my back. When I am having a bad day, he prays with me. When I am having a good day, he celebrates with me. That's what real, authentic friends do! You can be a real friend. Get over the culture of networking — following people just so you can get the hookup of your dreams. You're better than that! Friendship is way better than networking. Be a real friend; don't just say things, do things!

Be Authentic

One of the craziest stories in the Bible, in my opinion, is in Acts 19. It tells the story of a church leader named Sceva. You thought my name was crazy? How about being named Sceva (that's pronounced SKEEVA.) Actually, that's pretty cool, I guess. I met a kid the other day named Ocean. I think that's actually pretty cool and unique.

Anyway, if you read in Acts 19, you'll find that Sceva had some sons, and his sons tried to cast some dark spirits out of some people. The kingdom of darkness is a very real kingdom, and demons and dark spirits definitely do exist, even to this day. Sceva's sons — we don't even get to know their names — tried to cast some demons out of a man. As they tried to order the spirits to leave, one of the evil spirits talked back to them. The spirit said, in essence, "I know about Jesus, and I've even heard about Paul, but I don't know who you are." Next, the Bible records that the crazed man doesn't stop there. Turns out he was more action than talk. He goes crazy and beats the crap out of Sceva's sons, ripping their clothes off them and leaving them naked and bloody.

What a crazy scene that must have been! A wild man tearing these other people's clothes off them and beating the mess out of them in broad daylight, in public, in front of everyone!

I think it boils down to authenticity, though; I really do! Sceva's sons were around the things of God a lot. Sceva was a high priest. He knew Scriptures. He was supposed to be a person who lived a pure life. But when it came down to it, his sons just weren't authentic. You know, people can tell when we are not authentic. It's not easy to hide for long. You can't fake being something that you're not for too long. You might do it for a thirty-minute meeting or an hour-long event, but you can't wear that mask for too long without the real you coming out.

The fact of the matter is, however, that if you try to accomplish your life's missions, your dreams, and your plans by being someone you're not—if you try to meet your goals by being fake—you will always get your butt kicked. At the end of the day, you will always be empty. You will never know who you are. People will see right through your act. This is why I so firmly believe in being yourself, being who God made you to be.

Dare to be different and stand out. You cannot just talk the talk of faith, but you also have to walk the walk of faith, even when it's hard and you might not love who you are. When times are trying and you're not sure if your dreams are ever going to come to pass, keep walking the walk of faith. Keep loving people. Keep being authentic. Nobody wants to get their butt kicked. Do you really want to end up bloodied and naked? Authenticity will save you so much heartache and pain in life. Just be authentic, and just be you!

"Dare to be different and stand out."

Chapter 8 Discussion

1) Are there some random relationships in your life that you have a hard time explaining?

2) What are some ways you build relationships with others?

3) What is your take on friendship and networking? Have you benefited from either? How so?

4) When was a time that you were not authentic? Do you remember the outcome?

Final Thoughts

You are much too special and important to compare yourself to other people. You are too valuable to live with insecurities. There is too much at stake for your life. There are great things you must do. There are people in the world you must reach and places you must go and visit. Don't worry, though, you can do it. You will do it. We can be truly happy with who God made us to be and we can walk confidently in our talents, abilities, and gifts. We will work hard, and we will happily reach our dreams, living fulfilled lives. You matter. You're important.

> **"You are much too special and important to compare yourself to other people."**

In a sky full of stars, God saw you, chose you, placed you, and named you. He believes in you. He's cheering you on from heaven. He's yelling your name out and smiling like a big awkward dad at a soccer game. He loves you no matter what, and so do I.

If you don't have a personal relationship with Jesus Christ, what are you waiting on? It's not just life, it's life to the fullest potential. It's a crazy rollercoaster ride, and you'll never regret it. In Jesus your gifts and talents can flow and find meaning. In him your purpose in life is unlocked and you're given the major key to your destiny.

If you feel comfortable, pray this prayer out loud or to yourself:

God, I am giving my life to you! I am starting brand new with you today. I want to live for you. I want to get to know you. I want to delight in your Word and what it says about my life and me. I thank you for sending your son Jesus to die for me so that I don't have to live like a slave to my insecurities. Help me, Holy Spirit. Change my thinking. Change me daily!

In Jesus' name. Amen.

The Bible says if you believe Jesus did what he did (died a death to save us all) and why he did it (to set us right with the Father) and you share this good news with others, you're saved!

It's the word of faith that welcomes God to go to work and set things right for us. This is the core of our preaching. Say the welcoming word to God – "Jesus is my Master" – embracing, body and soul, God's work of doing in us what he did raising Jesus from the dead. That's it. You're not "doing" anything; you're simply calling out to God, trusting him to do it for you. That's salvation. With your whole being you embrace God setting things right, and then you say it, right out loud: "God has set everything right between him and me!"
—Romans 10:9-10 (MSG)

I want to challenge you. Following Jesus isn't a one-night-stand, hit-it-and-quit-it type of relationship. It's a marriage, one not meant to be broken or backed out of. Don't quit on him. Choose to love him, follow him daily, and seek his will and plans for your life.

You'll be faced every day with new opportunities to compare yourself to others or let your insecurities overtake you. Get closer to Jesus and live your own beautiful journey!

Chrétien Dumond is compassionate, creative, and completely original. Inspired by the tragedy comparison has caused in his own life, Chrétien spends his time encouraging others to be the original, unique individuals that God created them to be. Born and raised in Jacksonville, FL. Chrétien and his wife Mallory live in Eastern North Carolina where he spends much of his time mentoring young people, serving his city, working retail, substitute teaching, and volunteering in the youth ministry his wife pastors.

Connect
With
Chrétien

 facebook.com/chretiendumondonline

 @ChretienDumond

 @ChretienDumond

 @ChretienDumond

 P.O. Box 392 Goldsboro, NC 27533

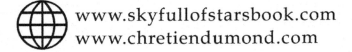 www.skyfullofstarsbook.com
www.chretiendumond.com

CPSIA information can be obtained
at www.ICGtesting.com
Printed in the USA
BVOW06s2154200217
476699BV00003B/5/P